CU00842036

# LESS PANIC

# MORE HOPE

*God's Promises and
Prayers to Overcome Fear,
Anxiety, and Depression*

**Daniel C. Okpara**

# Praying the

# Promises of God

# (Book 6)

**Copyright © August 2018 by Daniel C. Okpara**

All Rights Reserved. Kindly note that contents of this book should not be reproduced in any way or by any means without obtaining written consent from the author or his representative. However, brief excerpts for church or Christian references can be used without written permission.

Published By:

**Better Life Media.**

BETTER LIFE WORLD OUTREACH CENTER.

Website: www.BetterLifeWorld.org

Email: info@betterlifeworld.org

**FOLLOW US ON FACEBOOK**

1. Like our Page on Facebook for updates

2. Join Our Facebook Prayer Group, submit prayer requests and follow powerful daily prayers for total victory and breakthrough

Any scripture quotation used in this book is taken from the New King James Version, except where stated. Used by permission.

# Table of Contents

# RECEIVE DAILY AND WEEKLY PRAYERS

---

## Powerful Prayers Sent to Your Inbox Every Monday

Enter your email address to receive notifications of new posts, prayers and prophetic declarations sent to you by email.

Email Address

Sign Me Up

*Go to: **BreakThroughPrayers.org** to subscribe to receive FREE WEEKLY PRAYER POINTS, and prophetic declarations sent to you by email.*

# FREE BOOKS

Download These 4 Powerful Books Today for FREE... Take Your Relationship With God to a New Level.

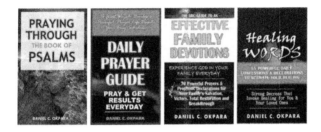

www.betterlifeworld.org/grow

# INTRODUCTION

More people (than we know) worldwide have a mental illness - such as depression, anxiety, fear, schizophrenia, eating disorders, and other addictive behaviors. In my ministry to others, it has remained one of the most challenging situations to handle. It's actually a more severe issue than we know. The World Health Organization (WHO) says that it is a leading cause of disability globally. Many sufferers do not have access to treatment and may not, in fact, know exactly what they are suffering from. But their health and life continue to get worse by the day.

Some common signs of mental or emotional illnesses include:

- Constant feeling of sadness

- Confused thinking or reduced ability to concentrate

- Unwarranted fears, worries, or extreme feelings of guilt

- Life-threatening mood changes of highs and lows

- Withdrawal from friends and social activities

- Extreme overtiredness, low energy, or constant difficulty in sleeping.

- Removal from reality (delusions), paranoia or illusions

- Inability to cope with day to day problems or stress

- Trouble relating to situations and people

- Alcohol or drug abuse

- Major changes in eating habits

- Sex drive changes

- Too much anger, hostility or violence

- Unnatural suicidal thoughts

- Sometimes sufferers experience stomach pain, back pain, headache, or other unexplained aches and pains.

Why do people have a mental illness?

Medical research does not know precisely what causes mental illness. They suggest it could be a result of genetic factors, environmental exposure (stress, provocative conditions, toxins, alcohol or drugs) or unidentified brain chemical reactions. However, I'd like to add that mental illnesses or emotional breakdown may also be caused by:

- Events that caused grief

- Loss of loved one

- Decreased satisfaction of life

- Family fights

- Difficulty in one's relationships and marriage

- Legal and financial problems

- Social separation

- Poverty, lack, and homelessness

- Inability to achieve goals

- Failure to receive answers to prayers

- And so on.

In this book, **_Less Panic More Hope_**, my goal is to speak healing and restoration to your mind. I want to show you that there is hope, and that life has excellent opportunities for you irrespective of what you have gone through. I want to help you identify your fears, worries, anxieties, depressions, and other mental and emotional challenges you have right now, and deal with them with God's word. I want to encourage you to take your discouragements, anxieties, fears, and disappointments to God in prayer and experience His peace that passes understanding. I believe that God's word and prayer will bring anyone total healing and restoration from mental or emotional afflictions.

*Mental illness is not a sign that one is weak. It is not a sign of a lack of spirituality. We live in a world bereft of hope, and mental illness is the emotional product of that reality.* Consequently, the only thing that will bring about reasonable, or total change, and healing of mental illness and change one's life sufficiently is God's hope and His Word of faith. The solution is to get God's confidence back inside of you.

# Chapter 1: Dealing With Fear

---

*"For God hath not given us the spirit of fear; but of power, and of love, and of a sound mind." - 2 Timothy 1:7*

---

God did not give you the spirit of fear – but of power, of love and of a sound mind. So if you're suffering from fear, you can be sure that it's not one of the gifts from God. It's from the devil. You have to reject it and send it back to where it's coming from.

Fear is a feeling prompted by perceived danger or threat that occurs, which causes a change in behavior, such as fleeing, hiding, or freezing from observed disturbing events. Fear may arise in response to a specific stimulus happening in the present, or in expectation of a coming threat seen as a risk to life.

Sometimes fear may be a rational, natural escape response to danger in our environments. But what happens when it is something more than usual, when it is felt when getting into the car, leaving the house, or being in a crowd? Are these feelings of fear okay?

The answer is no!

---

*When fear becomes tormenting, it does not come from God. Such emotions of fear can be the work of the spirit of fear.*

---

There are many things that people can be afraid of, but these are the most common phobias that mental health experts look for:

- **Social phobia:** An anxiety disorder which includes excessive worry in social situations.

- **Agoraphobia:** A fear of coming out in the open, feeling that something terrible will happen if one leaves the house and goes out, usually about specific places or venues.

- **Acrophobia:** A fear of heights

- **Pteromerhanophobia:** A fear of flying

- **Claustrophobia:** A fear of enclosed spaces

- **Entomophobia:** A fear of insects

- **Thanatophobia:** The fear of death

- **Necrophobia:** A fear of dying people or dead things

- **Ophidiophobia:** A fear of snakes

- **Cynophobia:** A fear of dogs

- **Astraphobia:** A fear of storms

- **Trypanophobia:** A fear of needles

Apart from these medically recognized fears and phobias, there are other types of fears that we can unconsciously nurture in our hearts. The Bible recognizes these fears and counsels us to reject them in our minds. They are:

1. The fear of losing your salvation

2. **The fear of danger** (Psalm 91:5): that is, being always afraid that something terrible will happen, either of accidents, robberies, disaster, and so on.

3. **The fear of death** (Hebrews 2:14-15): that is, being overly concerned and scared of death, so much as to want to do things to be protected

4. **The fear of criticism:** being over mindful of what people will say, to the extent of delaying or avoiding necessary actions in one's life

5. **The fear of people's threats** (Proverbs 29:25): such that one is not able to be himself or stand for the truth.

6. **The fear of failing in business and investment** (Ecclesiastes 11:4)**:** being afraid of investing, or losing money in a project. This can make one become too careful and never want to retake future business risks.

7. **The fear of illness** (1 Peter 2:24): either of an epidemic or not recovering from an illness

8. **The fear of demons** (1 John 4:4): fear of witches, fear of curses, and evil powers; not trusting that God does protect from demonic forces.

9. **The fear of possible disappointment in marriage** (Matthew 19:4-6): being consumed with thoughts of divorce; always thinking: *my marriage is crashing;*

*my spouse is cheating*, etc. even when there are no reasons for that).

10. **The fear of what the future holds** (Jeremiah 29:11): always worried about uncertainty of tomorrow

11. **The fear of old age** (Psalm 92:12-14): fear of losing health or beauty as one age; fear of being alone and unloved.

12. **The fear of losing your job**


## GOD'S ANSWERS TO FEAR

Do you see yourself having any of these fears? Are there other fears not mentioned that unsuspectingly crawl into your mind a few times? It's time to recognize these fears and confront them with God's words.

The Bible contains almost 400 admonitions on fear. When you feel dazed with fear, read these scriptures and turn them into prayers.

## 1. God is With You

Isaiah 41:10 –*Fear not, for I am with you; be not dismayed, for I am your God. I will strengthen you, yes, I will help you, and I will uphold you with my righteous right hand.*

Isaiah 45:2-3 - *I will go before you and make the crooked places straight; I will break in pieces the gates of bronze and cut the bars of iron. I will give you the treasures of darkness and hidden riches of secret places, that you may know that*

*I, the Lord, who call you by your name, am the God of Israel.*

**Hebrews 13:6** - *So we may boldly say: 'The Lord is my helper; I will not fear. What can man do to me?'*

## 2. God is greater than your fears

**Psalm 5:11** - But let all those rejoice who put their trust in You; let them ever shout for joy, because You defend them; let those also who love Your name be joyful in You.

**Psalm 56:11** - In God, I have put my trust; I will not be afraid. What can man do to me?

**Proverbs 29:5** - The fear of man brings a snare, but whoever trusts in the Lord shall be safe.

Matthew 10:31 - Do not fear therefore; you are of more value than many sparrows.

## 3. Whatever It is, God Will Fight for You

Exodus 14:14 - *The Lord will fight for you, and you shall hold your peace.*

2 Chronicles 32:7 - *Be strong and courageous; do not be afraid nor dismayed before the king of Assyria, nor before the entire multitude that is with him; for there are more with us than with him.*

Proverbs 20:22 - *Do not say, 'I will recompense evil'; wait for the Lord, and He will save you.*

Isaiah 49:25 - *Thus says the Lord: 'Even the captives of the mighty shall be taken away, and the prey of the terrible be delivered; for I will contend with him who contends with you, and I will save your children.*

Deuteronomy 3:22 - *You must not fear them, for the Lord your God Himself fights for you.*

Psalm 35:1-3 - *Plead my cause, O Lord, with those who strive with me; fight against those who fight against me. Take hold of shield and buckler, and stand up for my help. Also, draw out the spear, and stop those who pursue me. Say to my soul, "I am your salvation."*

## 4. Your fears are not of God

2 Timothy 1:7 - *For God has not given us a spirit of fear but of power and love and a sound mind.*

1 John 4:18 - *There is no fear in love, but perfect love casts out fear because fear involves torment. But he who fears has not been made perfect in love.*

## 5. Pray and Seek God if you are afraid

Psalm 34:4 - *I sought the Lord, and He heard me and delivered me from all my fears.*

Psalm 55:22 - *Cast your burden on the Lord, and he shall sustain you; he shall never permit the righteous to be moved.*

Philippians 4:6-7 - *Be anxious for nothing, but in everything by prayer and supplication, with thanksgiving, let your requests be made known to God; and the peace of God, which surpasses all understanding, will guard your hearts and minds through Christ Jesus.*

*1 Peter 5:6-7 - Therefore humble yourselves under the mighty hand of God, that He may exalt you in due time, 7 casting all your care upon Him, for He cares for you.*

## 6. No matter what happens, God is in control

Matthew 24:6 - *And you will hear of wars and rumors of wars. See that you are not troubled; for all these things must come to pass, but the end is not yet.*

Psalm 46:1-3 - God is our refuge and strength, a very present help in trouble. Therefore we will not fear, even though the earth be removed, and though the mountains be carried into the midst of the sea; though its waters roar and be troubled, though the mountains shake with its swelling.

**Psalm 91:5-7** - *You shall not be afraid of the terror by night, nor of the arrow that flies by day, ₆ nor of the pestilence that walks in darkness, nor of the destruction that lays waste at noonday. ₇A thousand may fall at your side, and ten thousand at your right hand; but it shall not come near you. ₈Only with your eyes shall you look, and see the reward of the wicked.*

**Psalm 94:19** - In the multitude of my anxieties within me, your comforts delight my soul.

**1 Corinthians 10:13** - *No temptation has overtaken you except such as is common to man; but God is faithful, who will not allow you to be tempted beyond what you are able, but with the temptation will also make the way of escape, that you may be able to bear it.*

# PRAYING THROUGH YOUR FEAR

Here are practical steps to overcome any fear resting in your mind and troubling your life at the moment.

## 1. Identify What You're Afraid of

Let's do some work.

What are the things you fear?

It's possible that what gets you afraid in life or bother your peace of mind is in the twelve fears stated above. It's also possible that your fears are not stated here. Try, however, to look deep and identify the real issues you fear the most. Take a piece of paper and list the things that seem to border and get you scared. Once we can pinpoint these issues, we can now deal with them appropriately.

## 2. Seek God in Prayer

There was a time in David's life that circumstances and adverse events pressed him so hard that he developed fears all around. He became unsure if God was still with him. What did he do? How did he handle such moments in his life?

He said: ***"I sought the LORD, and He delivered me from all my fears"*** – Psalm 34:4

He Sought God in prayers, and He delivered him from ***"all his fears!"*** Not one, not two, not three. They must have been so many.

It's possible that we suddenly begin to have fears in our hearts due to the way things are going in the home, in the office or the nation. It's possible that our fears are justifiable. But the truth is that these fears do not eventually produce good fruits.

Whenever you notice that you are developing fears all around, probably because of disappointments, frustrations, delayed answers to prayers, or others, your next best action should be to declare a season of rest in God's presence until your confidence and faith are completely restored.

This rest could be a season of fasting and prayers or personal retreat to read the Bible and meditate.

It's crucial that you don't get carried away with being busy, ignore your fears and live like all is well. Don't. Take some time out and deal with your fears and let God restore your confidence and direction. God said: *"Call to me and I will answer you and tell you great and unsearchable things you do not know."*– Jeremiah 33:3

## 3. Start Rejecting *Fear Inviting Words*

Words are spiritual forces that create physical realities. Just as the Israelites bought their fear and defeat through the words they heard from Goliath, we can also let fear into our hearts by the words we hear. These words may be the news we watch, what the doctors are saying, what neighbors think and say about us, what teachers say about our children, and so on.

To continue to manifest victory over fear, worry, and depression, we must learn how to reject news and words that build up our fears about those things we fear. Just as faith comes from WORDS (of GOD), fear also comes through WORDS (Romans 10:17).

Jesus already said that in the world there will be a lot of tribulations, but that we have peace in Him. Prophet Isaiah also said that gross darkness will cover the earth and the peoples, but that our light will shine (Isaiah 60:1-3). So when men come up with their analyses on how terrible things are going to become, how bad one's health will be, or how the kids aren't doing great, we should find rest in God's WORDS and reject all of the bad news in our spirits.

## 4. Speak to Yourself

No one doesn't come to a point in life when fear and worry is justifiable. However, how we handle such moments makes all the difference. When you're faced with situations that nurture fear, spend time to speak to yourself morning and night. Read some of the scriptures above and use them for personal self-speaking. As you consistently talk to yourself with God's words, these fears will leave, and you'll have the energy to face what's happening and receive grace to overcome.

# QUESTIONS

## 1. What are the things you're afraid of? List them below

..............................................................

..............................................................

..............................................................

## 2. What will you do today to address these fears?

..............................................................

..............................................................

..............................................................

# DECLARATION

*"God is with me; I will not be afraid. He is my helper, upholder, and protector. He will strengthen me and help me at all times."*

# Chapter 2: Dealing With Worry and Anxiety

---

*"People become attached to their burdens sometimes more than the burdens are attached to them."* –

**George Bernard Shaw**

---

Let's face it. Each of us worries about something at some point. When the rent is due, and the money is not available, we think about it. We worry about how to raise the money.

Yes, everybody, both adults, and children, experiences worry (or anxiety) from time to time. For most persons, feelings of worry come and go, only lasting a short time. However, when worry becomes too frequent, it drives people into a lingering state of nervousness and fear, leading to what experts call anxiety disorder.

Worry and anxiety have been linked to multiple protracted health conditions including heart disease, abdominal problems, and breathing ailments. It is also a contributor to substance misuse because many people who suffer from anxiety conditions tend to turn to alcohol or drugs to calm or numb their nervous feelings.

But a life spent in a persistent state of anxiousness doesn't have to be.

Some studies suggest that one in every thirteen people are suffering from anxiety, while nearly 300 million people are affected worldwide. It is a significant source of mental and health breakdown.

# TYPES OF ANXIETY

When treating anxiety, mental health experts look for the following anxieties.

## 1. Generalized anxiety disorder (GAD)

This type of anxiety is characterized by persistent and extreme worry about different things, like worrying about money issues, worrying about aging, worrying about health, worrying about family, work, clothes, children, or other problems. Sometimes sufferers worry more than warranted about actual events or may expect the worst even when there is no real reason for such worries. GAD is the primary type of anxiety disorder often identified with people. No wonder Jesus warned against it in His message to us. He said:

*₂₅ Therefore I tell you, do not worry about your life, what you will eat or drink; or about your body, what you will wear. Is not life more than food, and the body more than clothes? ₂₆ Look at the birds of the air; they do not sow or reap or store away in barns, and yet your heavenly Father feeds them. Are you not much more valuable than they? ₂₇ Can anyone of you by worrying add a single hour to your life?*

*₂₈ And why do you worry about clothes? See how the flowers of the field grow. They do not labor or spin. ₂₉ I tell you that not even Solomon in all his splendor was dressed like one of these. ₃₀ If that is how God clothes the grass of the field, which is here today and tomorrow is thrown into the fire, will he not much more clothe you-you of little faith?*

*₃₁ So do not worry, saying, 'What shall we eat?' or 'What shall we drink?' or 'What shall we wear?'*

*₃₂ For the pagans run after all these things, and your heavenly Father knows that you need them. ₃₃ But seek first his kingdom and his righteousness, and all these things will be given to you as well. ₃₄ Therefore do not worry about tomorrow, for tomorrow will worry about itself. Each day has enough trouble of its own.*

Jesus is saying that worrying about things will not solve the problems. It will instead compound them.

So a right way to help yourself when you unconsciously want to worry about these numerous issues and challenges of life is to think this way:

*"My worry will not help me. I will rather seek the kingdom of God. His peace and clarity will give me the strength to think and know what to do. So I refuse to worry."*

Confront your urge to worry as a fight, and refuse to stop challenging your mind until anxiety leaves.

## 2. Panic Disorder

The *Anxiety and Depression Association of America* (ADAA) defines panic disorder as the sudden, repeated bouts of forceful fear, discomfort, or terror that peak in a matter of minutes. Some of the symptoms include: trembling or shaking, feelings of choking, shivers, pounding heart, sweating, chills or heat sensations, feelings of looming danger, shortness of breath, chest pain, feelings of losing oneself, etc. Panic disorder simply means suddenly getting afraid and frightened from time to time.

As I've noted earlier, you don't have to let fear and panic become a part of you. When you're about to panic over anything, you can declare and say:

---

*"No way! God has not given me the spirit of fear or panic. I have the spirit of love, of power, and of a sound mind. So I won't let fear and panic rule my mind and life, in Jesus name"*

---

Do not approach these situations with soft handedness. They can be a source of big problems in your life if not dealt with.

## 3. Obsessive-Compulsive Disorder (OCD)

According to *AnxietyBC.com*, an online portal that provides information, resources, and tools to help with anxiety, Obsessive Compulsive Disorder (OCD) is the invasion of unwanted and troubling thoughts, images, or urges (obsessions) that intrude into an individual's mind and cause a great deal of anxiety or distress, which the person then tries to ease by engaging in repetitive behaviors (compulsions). A person may know these thoughts are unimportant, but they will try to relieve their anxiety by performing certain rituals or practices. This may include hand washing, counting, or checking on things such as whether or not they've locked their house.

Apostle Paul understood the threat of harmful thought invasions and recommended that we arrest them with prayers. He sees them as a war on our soul, and that's precisely what they are.

*₃For though we live in the flesh as mortal men, we are not carrying on our warfare according to the flesh and using the weapons of man. ₄The weapons of our warfare are not physical weapons of flesh and blood. Our weapons are divinely powerful for the destruction of fortresses.*

*₅We are destroying sophisticated arguments and every exalted and proud thing that sets itself up against the true knowledge of God, and we are taking every thought and purpose captive to the obedience of Christ* (2 Corinthians 10:3-7 – AMP).

Do not assume that when these so-called negative and evil thoughts invade your mind, they are normal and ordinary. No. They are demonic projections with the intention to ruin your life. Attack them with prayers and command your mind to rest in God's protective ability.

## 4. Post-Traumatic Stress Disorder (PTSD)

Posttraumatic stress disorder (PTSD) is a severe mental condition that some people develop after a shocking, terrifying, or dangerous event. It is characterized by failure to recover after experiencing or witnessing a scary incident, such as war, assault, natural disaster, accident, loss of a loved one, or other related happenings. These events are called traumas.

God's truth is the key to coping with or overcoming PTSD. Reminding oneself that God loves, forgives, and cares for His people is extremely important. Sometimes, we will not be able to understand it all, but God is working even in the circumstances.

Yes, it's not easy what has happened, and things will take time to normalize again. But all things are working together for our good. Constantly remind yourself that:

*"Yes, I may not understand everything. But God is good, and He will see me through."*

## 5. Social Anxiety Disorder

Social Anxiety Disorder (SAD), also known as social phobia, is characterized by great fear in one or more social situations. It is an intense worry of being judged, negatively assessed, or rejected by people. This may lead to avoiding social gatherings, and when a situation cannot be avoided, can lead to serious distress.

## 6. Agoraphobia

Agoraphobia is the dread of being in a situation from which one either cannot escape or from which escaping would be tough or uncomfortable. People with agoraphobia may try to avoid these places and situations to prevent panic attacks.

Whatever anxiety one is suffering from, the goal of anxiety is the same: *to steal, kill and destroy.* Yes, anxiety is Satan's tool for accomplishing his purpose of destruction. It is therefore essential to recognize your anxiety and deal with it.

## CAUSES OF ANXIETY

Medical experts don't completely understand what causes anxiety disorders. It's currently believed that certain traumatic experiences can trigger anxiety in people who are prone to it. Genetics may also play a role in anxiety. In many cases, the following external factors are responsible:

- Pressure at work or school

- Pressure in a relationship, e.g.: unstable marriage, divorce, or misbehaving children

- Financial stress

- Pressure from the death of a loved one

- Severe illness (or symptoms of perceived severe medical conditions)

- A side effect of medication

- Genetic factors

- Use of an illegal drugs

- Traumatic experiences, such as war, assault, domestic violence, natural disaster, accident, loss of property, legal issues, debt, or other related events

- Unfulfilled expectations

- Unanswered Prayers

Many factors, both known and unknown, can be responsible for anxiety and worry. The essential thing, however, is to recognize that anxiety is not a good friend. It is an enemy and must be sent packing.

## A LITTLE SELF EXAMINATION

Anxiety may present itself as worry about a looming event or situation. You may be nervous or overly disturbed and even fearful. This thing, whatever it is, sticks in your mind and it begins to take over your life when left unchecked. It is not a place that anyone wants to be, but a place that we can easily find ourselves when thinking about the wrong things.

The first thing you may want to do to reclaim your mind from worry and anxiety is to ask a few questions, like:

- "What am I apprehensive and anxious about?" List the things that get you anxious and worrisome.
- "By getting worried about these things, how have I solved the problems?" Be honest.
- "How is my worry and anxiety about these things affecting my health, relationships, and behavior?" Be open to yourself, and you'll be shocked at your finding.

Once you have identified your worries and its effects on your attitude, relationships, and health, it's now time to do battle with the WORD of God. Banish the evil spirits attacking your mind with anxiety and worry.

# PRAYING GOD'S WORD TO DEAL WITH ANXIETY

The scriptures below contain God's promises for you to use and pray against worry and anxiety. Personalize these scriptures and promises. Meditate on them and speak them to yourself. God's power will set you free from anxiety.

There is a short prayer after each scripture. Use these prayers to pray these promises into your heart, and to receive deliverance from anxiety problems. Always remember that the Word of God, His hope, is the cure for mental issues.

## 1. GOD WILL TAKE CARE OF YOU

**Matthew 6:25-34 (TLB)** - *Don't worry about things—food, drink, and clothes. For you already have life and a body—*

*and they are far more important than what to eat and wear. Look at the birds! They don't worry about what to eat—they don't need to sow or reap or store up food—for your heavenly Father feeds them. And you are far more valuable to him than they are.*

***Will all your worries add a single moment to your life?*** *And why worry about your clothes? Look at the field lilies! They don't worry about theirs. Yet King Solomon in all his glory was not clothed as beautifully as they. And if God cares so wonderfully for flowers that are here today and gone tomorrow, won't he more surely care for you, O men of little faith?*

*So don't worry at all about having enough food and clothing. Why be like the heathen? For they take pride in all these things and are deeply concerned about them. But your heavenly Father already knows perfectly well that you need them, 33 and he will give them to you if you give him first place in your life and live as he wants you to.*

*"So don't be anxious about tomorrow. God will take care of your tomorrow too. Live one day at a time.*

## PRAY

*Father in the name of Jesus Christ, I refuse to worry about food, drink, and clothes from this day forward. And I give You praise for the gift of life and health. As long as I have breath, health and continue to follow You, I know You will always provide for me.*

*You, LORD, feed the birds of the air and clothe the grass of the field, how much more will you provide for us who put our trust in You.*

*Please, Lord, forgive me for having allowed worry and anxiety to rest in my heart. Forgive me for thinking too little of You and for not trusting You always.*

*From this day, Lord, I rest in Your promise to take care of me. I know that my tomorrow is secure in You. I know that You will see me through always.*

*In Jesus name, I pray.*

## 2. DON'T BE AFRAID

**Deuteronomy 31:8** - *And the Lord, He is the One who goes before you. He will be with you; He will not leave you nor forsake you; do not fear nor be dismayed.*

**Proverbs 29:25** - *The fear of man brings a snare, but whoever trusts in the Lord shall be safe.*

**Isaiah 43:1-2** - *But now, thus says the Lord, who created you, O Jacob, and He who formed you, O Israel: "Fear not, for I have redeemed you; I have called you by your name; you are Mine. When you pass through the waters, I will be with you; and through the rivers, they shall not overflow you. When you walk through the fire, you shall not be burned, nor shall the flame scorch you.*

**Isaiah 41:10** - *Fear not, for I am with you; be not dismayed, for I am your God. I will strengthen you, yes, I will help you, I will uphold you with My righteous right hand.'*

**Romans 8:15** - *For you did not receive the spirit of bondage again to fear, but you received the Spirit of adoption by whom we cry out, "Abba, Father."*

**2 Timothy 1:7** - *For God has not given us a spirit of fear, but of power and of love and of a sound mind.*

**Psalm 34:3-4** - *Oh, magnify the Lord with me, and let us exalt His name together. I sought the Lord, and He heard me and delivered me from all my fears.*

# PRAY

*Father, Lord, I thank You for giving me the Spirit of love, of power and of a sound mind. Thank You for giving me freedom in Christ and delivering me from the bondage of fear and panic.*

*Lord, I know that You are at work in my life every day; I know that You will go before me in all my ways; You will be with me; You will not leave me nor forsake me.*

*I declare today that I will not be afraid, for You, God, is with me. When I pass through the waters, You will be with me; and through the rivers, they shall not overflow me. When I walk through the fire, I shall not be burned, nor shall the flame scorch me.*

*I, therefore, bind the spirit of fear and panic in my life and cast them out in Jesus name. I pull myself out of every trap I have entered due to fear and panic.*

*I declare that I put my trust in the Lord; therefore, I shall be safe and protected from all forms of trouble and danger.*

*I will magnify the Lord and exalt His name forever because He has heard me, and delivered me from all my fears.*

*In Jesus name, I pray*

## 3. COMMAND WORRY AND ANXIETY TO LEAVE

**Proverbs 12:25** - *Anxiety in a man's heart weighs him down, but a good word makes him glad.*

**Proverbs 17:22** – *A joyful heart is good medicine, but a crushed spirit dries up the bones.*

**Philippians 4:6-7** – *Do not be anxious about anything, but in everything by prayer and supplication with thanksgiving let your requests be made known to God. And the peace of God, which surpasses all understanding, will guard your hearts and your minds in Christ Jesus.*

**1 Peter 5:6-7** - *Humble yourselves, therefore, under the mighty hand of God so that at the proper time he may exalt you, casting all your anxieties on him, because he cares for you.*

**Psalm 94:19** (TLB) – *Lord, when doubts fill my mind, when my heart is in* *turmoil, quiet me and give me renewed hope and cheer.*

**Romans 8:26-28** (TLB) *– And in the same way—by our faith—the Holy Spirit helps us with our daily problems and in our praying. For we don't even know what we should pray for nor how to pray as we should, but the Holy Spirit prays for us with such feeling that it cannot be expressed in words.*

*And the Father who knows all hearts knows, of course, what the Spirit is saying as he pleads for us in harmony with God's own will. And we know that all that happens to us is working for our good if we love God and are fitting into his plans.*

**2 Corinthians** 4:17 - *For this light momentary affliction is preparing for us* an eternal weight of glory beyond all comparison

## PRAY

*Heavenly Father, I humble myself before You this day and cast all my anxieties on You. I know that You care for me, and You are at work in my life.*

*Lord, I praise You because everything that has happened to me is working out for my good. Yes, Lord, You will use everything to work out good in my life. So I praise You forever and ever, in Jesus name.*

*I pray today, Lord, when doubts fill my mind, when my heart is in confusion, quiet me and give me renewed hope and cheer. And let Your peace which surpasses all understanding guard my heart and my mind in Christ Jesus.*

*Clothe me with confidence, faith and supernatural joy that recognizes that You are always in control, in Jesus name.*

*I speak to myself henceforth to rest in the Lord and in His precious promises. He will not let me down or allow me to be broken.*

*I speak to the demons of worry and anxiety to leave my life and never return, in Jesus name.*

*I claim complete restoration in my health, finances, and family. I claim restoration in every aspect of my life. In Jesus name.*

*Amen.*

# CONTINUALLY DECLARE
# SCRIPTURES TO YOURSELF

Once in a while, one's mind may become disturbed over the state of things as they are at the moment. Sometimes, you may become bothered about life and situation of things. You may become unhappy with yourself and where you are at present. Now, this state of thought, at first, is healthy, especially if it leads you to reassess everything and decide to make changes.

But when it stays longer than necessary, it may degenerate into feelings of regret, fear, depression, and anxiety about tomorrow. To properly handle such moments, learn to speak scripture words to yourself.

Speaking scripture-words to yourself is the best way to defeat the demons of worry and anxiety from time to time. This is what you do: you read the scriptures and God's promises such as presented above. Then you begin to personalize the words to yourself. For example, taking Isaiah 41:10, you'll say to yourself:

---

*"I will not fear or be troubled because God is with me. He will strengthen me and help me. He will uphold me with His hand of love."*

---

Taking Psalm 55, you'll say to yourself: *"I'm casting this burden to the LORD. He's going to sustain me.*

### *He'll never allow me to be moved or shaken."*

As you speak scripture words to yourself, the power of God is released, and your heart is calmed. Then you'll be able to receive God's ideas and revelations for moving forward.

You may not be feeling spiritual as you're speaking the Word. But we're not to be led by our feelings. The Word works whether we have some exciting spiritual feelings or not.

The truth is that no matter how bad things are, getting worried and anxious does not produce any progress or resolve the challenges that is confronting you at the moment.

Anxiety and worry only expand the situation and problems, because it affects your health. Leo F. Buscaglia said, "Worry never robs tomorrow of its sorrow, it only saps today of its joy."

Stop giving the devil the opportunity to rob your peace of mind with unnecessary fears. Start dealing with yourself, your thoughts, and the demonic elements attacking your mind.

# QUESTIONS

## 1. Why are you worried? List your worries below

....................................................................

....................................................................

....................................................................

## 2. What will you do today to address these issues?

....................................................................

....................................................................

....................................................................

# DECLARATION

*"I speak to myself henceforth to rest in the Lord and in His precious promises. He is at work in my life and will provide for all my needs; He will not let me down, or allow me to be broken, in Jesus name."*

# Chapter 3: Dealing With Depression

*"Faith tells me that no matter what lies ahead of me, God is already there."* –Unknown

A few months ago, the media was jam-packed with the story of a young Deeper Life Doctor who committed suicide. The story shocked many people because they felt there was no reason for that. He lived in a highbrow area of the city where the well-to-do men and women live. He was a medical Doctor and in his early thirties, had a loving mother, an expensive car, a personal chauffeur, and worked in a semi-large hospital. He seemed to have life going for him. Yet he cruelly took his life by jumping into a lagoon after a Sunday service.

Why?

Depression.

"Depression," says WebMD, "...is an episode of sadness or apathy along with other symptoms that last at least two successive weeks and is severe enough to interrupt daily activities." It is a feeling of hopelessness (all hope is lost), despair, misery, dejection, and unhappiness that stays with one for an extended period."

Depression is a horrible thing. While some of it can be from genes, hormones, chemical imbalances or whatever, I believe the majority of depression is from the devil. Our minds are where he attacks us with feelings of guilt, anxiety, fear, self-pity, low self-esteem, and feelings of hopelessness.

32-year old Bill wrote for counseling and prayer support. Hear him:.

*"Hello,*

*I'm 32 years old, and for four months I suffer from a terrible depression. I don't know what to do; I feel hopeless, very scared and unable to feel happy again. I have never had such moods before in my life.*

*Once in a while, I was sad, of course, but it lasted a couple of days at most, and it wasn't that bad. Now it is different, I even have thoughts of suicide, but then I think of all the good things I have done and the nice things I have lived for (and all dreams that I had), that stops me from doing it.*

*I liked my life and how happy I was. I don't consider myself a bad person, but since I have fallen into this hole, I started thinking that I am selfish because of just thinking of my pain and being unhappy despite every blessings and love I have around me.*

*I am not married, and I do not have children, but I am in a 3-year relationship with a beautiful person who tries to help me as much as possible since my depression started. I don't want my treasured ones to suffer because of me, and I do not want anyone to bear this pain either. But it's too difficult to get over.*

*I started therapy already, and I am still searching the way to get through this. Sometimes it feels so unbearable that I just wish that the Lord takes me with him, but I don't want to leave all my dreams behind, and all the love I have found in my life. I consider I am too young for that. I am scared that someday I will think it is too much suffering that I will just take my own life. I am also frightened that this horrifying feeling will stay forever with me.*

*If someone out there has some advice, please share it with me. Tears drop down my face as I write this, I am desperate.*

*Thank you.*

You may spank Bill for getting depressed when he has almost everything going for him. But he is only one among the over 300 million people who have depression worldwide and struggle with it daily.

People who suffer from depression often are sad or uninterested in anything. Depressed people may sleep a lot and enjoy spending time in darkness, rather than the light.

Depression is not a sign of the absence of spirituality. Yes. It's not a sign that you're too worldly and unspiritual. As I said, we live in a world bereft of hope, and depression and other mental illnesses are the emotional product of that reality. The only thing that will change one's life sufficiently, as to destroy the root system, and effects of depression is God's hope and His Word of faith. The solution is to get God's confidence back inside of you.

## CAUSES OF DEPRESSION

A lot of things can cause depression, including, but not limited to illness, betrayal, unfulfilled expectations, divorce and marriage failure, accident, loss of a loved one, hardship, delayed answers to prayers, inability to get healed, and so on. The result of these experiences can lead one to be dejected.

However, God's hope will let you again see the *'future positive possibility'* of your life. It doesn't matter what's happening, or what has happened in your life; you can look forward and see that there is hope for you.

Accept God's hope which encourages, motivates, and keeps you on the road to faith, peace, and victory. The Word of God says...

> *"For to him that is joined to all the living there is hope: for a living dog is better than a dead lion."* -
> Ecclesiastes 9:4

As long as there is life, there is hope. Things will undoubtedly change for good. That's what the Word says.

Let me share the story of Sister Bliss (not her real name) with you. In her darkest moments of hopelessness, she found hope in God to live and fulfill God's plans for her life. She writes in her own words:

## "I PRAYED FOR HIM TO DIE.

*"Don't judge me; pause until you hear me out.*

*"He was a remarkable healthy child when I had him, but by age two, we noticed there was something wrong. There was no eye interaction; he could not talk, didn't understand instructions, and so many other bad vibes.*

*"That was when my nightmare started. I ran from place to place seeking a solution. In some places they said he was partially deaf, at others they said it was Autism. Up until then, I never heard the word Autism. The information I got about it was frightening, and I saw those signs clearly in my son.*

*"My life stood still.*

*"No school would take him as he couldn't settle. Finally, and luckily, an Indian lady with a nursery school took him in, but my heart broke the day I went to pick him up from school and asked her politely how he was doing. Her response was, 'I don't know what to do with him. I'm just a teacher, not a psychiatrist.'*

*"I cried all the way home. Thoughts bombarded my mind. Worst of it all, there was no answer to the tormenting thoughts.*

*"An only son, autism, was it generational? Or the devil?*

*"No answer!*

*"Up until then, I was having a swell time living my life to the fullest. But with this dilemma, I crawled to God. I attended every Christian gathering, crusade, vigils, name it.*

*"I prayed, prayed, cried, fasted, sowed seeds, but nothing happened.*

*"The years went by, and it outwardly got worse. People were beginning to notice there was a problem. I couldn't hide it anymore. (By the way, don't try hiding your shame. If God doesn't hide it, you can't hide it)*

*"My husband was tired. My mother who was perpetually encouraging me was tired; I was tired, exhausted and tired of casting, binding, fighting and 'faithing.' So, I prayed for him to die. I wanted to move on with my life. I wanted a shortcut.*

*"He didn't die. Instead, he grew. Seeing God wasn't ready to take him, I went back to God again in prayer; I repented and continued from where I stopped - running from church to church, from pillar to post.*

*"At one church, I was told to go on one week dry fast with consistent midnight prayers. At midnight when I came down to pray, I was*

*usually afraid. One night as I came down for the prayer routine, I heard a voice say to me,* **'How can you be praying and fearful? You are afraid because you don't know the God you are praying to***.'*

*"At that point, I packed up and went on a quest to know this GOD! I stayed alone for two weeks with only one prayer point –* **'God if you are real, let me know you.'** *I spent more time in those weeks studying the Word of God, and through the pages of the Bible, I came to know this GOD.*

**"After those two weeks of Word immersion, I had peace like I never had since the ordeal started. The burden for my son to talk or get normal left me. I came to peace with God and the World.**

*"About three weeks later, we traveled to England on Holiday. We were in a shop on Oxford Street when my son that had never*

*spoken came to me, tapped me, and asked a question.*

*"His first words to me were, 'where is Kamsy?'*

*"He was asking for his older sister. That was how my son started talking. One thing led to another, he began doing things he couldn't do and like magic caught up with his age mates.*

*"Yes, it was like Magic! No! A Miracle!*

*"Today I celebrate God as He turns 18. There is nothing we don't talk about now. From his school work to the girls that like him and the ones he likes. Sometimes I even scold him that he talks too much, correcting him that as a gentleman he shouldn't talk too much. How we so quickly forget!*

*"I can't thank God enough for him. Through my trial with him, I was reconnected back to God, I found my purpose in Life, and my ministry was birthed (That is another story for another Day).*

*"I encourage you today in your trial to fight on. No shortcut. God has not disappeared; take your eyes off your problem (if you can). Seek Him, and He will supply the lacking, plus much more*

Wow!

Indeed, *"weeping may endure for a night, but joy comes in the morning* (Psalm 30:5).

There are many things to take away from Sister Bliss' story:

1. Take your focus away from your situation for a moment and fix it steadily on God; you'll find great hope and encouragement.

2. God will show Himself to you as you genuinely seek him through His Word. His Word is Himself.

When you're feeling hopeless, and the devil is lying to your mind, seek God through His Word. You'll find hope in it, and you'll be revived again to live life and fulfill God's plan for your life.

## PRAYERS TO DEAL WITH DEPRESSION

God's Word is the pillar of hope and cure for depression. The scriptures below contain God's promises for you to use and pray against depression. They have been turned into prayers and meditations for you to speak to yourself and pray out loud. As you pray and declare these scriptures God's power will set you free from depression.

## God will deliver you from the troubles

Psalms 34:17–18 – The righteous cry and the LORD heareth, and delivereth them out of all their troubles. The LORD is near to them who are of a broken heart and saves such as be of a contrite spirit.

Psalm 34:19 (NIV) - The righteous person may have many troubles, but the LORD delivers him from them all.

Psalms 22:24 - For he has not despised or abhorred the affliction of the afflicted, and he has not hidden his face from him, but has heard, when he cried to him.

## PRAY:

*Father, I thank You because You have heard me and do know all my secret tears and pains, You will deliver me out of all my troubles; for You are near unto me, and will save me from whatever is upsetting me at the moment, in Jesus name.*

## God will give you rest

Matthew 11:28 – Come unto me, all ye that labor and are heavy laden, and I will give you rest.

**Psalms 116:1-2** - I love the Lord because he has heard my voice and my pleas for mercy. Because he inclined his ear to me, therefore I will call on him as long as I live.

## PRAY:

*It is to You O LORD that I pray and cry to. It is to You that my labor and pains are come to. You know everything about me, even more than I know myself.*

*You will give me rest according to Your Word; yes, Lord, may I receive Your rest today, May I receive your inner healing and peace that passes all understanding, in Jesus name.*

## Cast all your cares to the Lord

**1 Peter 5:7** - Casting all your care upon him; for he cares for you.

**Psalms 55:22** - Cast your burden on the LORD, and he will sustain you; he will never permit the righteous to be moved.

**Psalms 46:1** - God is our refuge and strength, a very present help in trouble.

## PRAY:

*Heavenly Father, I cast all my cares, worries and fears unto You today. I know that You care for me. I know that You will be with me always and will see me through all forms of predicaments. Shed Your love in my heart and restore my joy and confidence.*

*Sometimes, Lord, I allow myself to be caught up in self-pity, low self-esteem, inner guilt and sorrow about the past. I ask for Your help, Holy Spirit empowerment, and support to come out of these emotional travails. Inspire me with great songs of love and care, as I rest in your promises, in Jesus name.*

## Do not fear

**Isaiah 41:10** - Fear thou not; for I am with thee: be not dismayed; for I am thy God: I will strengthen thee; yea, I will help thee; yea, I will uphold thee with the right hand of my righteousness.

**2 Timothy 1:7** - For God hath not given us the spirit of fear; but of power, and of love, and of a sound mind.

## PRAY:

*Today, O Lord, I bind and cast out the spirits of fear, worry, and depression from my life, in Jesus name. I declare that I have boldness, confidence, and joy. God has not given me the spirit of fear, but of power, of love and of a sound mind.*

*Henceforth, Lord, I reject every attack on my mind. I declare that God is with me; He will uphold me with His righteous right hand, and I shall not be move, in the name of Jesus Christ.*

### God is with you

**Jeremiah 29:11** - For I know the thoughts that I think toward you, saith the

LORD, thoughts of peace, and not of evil, to give you an expected end.

**Psalms 23:4** - Yea, though I walk through the valley of the shadow of death, I will fear no evil: for thou art with me; thy rod and thy staff they comfort me.

## PRAY:

*O Lord, I thank You today because You have good plans for me. Your thoughts for me are peace and not evil, to give me hope and a good future. For this, I say thank You, Lord.*

*Lord, there are many times that my reason for worry, depression and unhappiness is a result of the situation of things in my life, the dangers I have gone through, and how tomorrow will eventually be. I worry and depress, feeling uncertain about my life and future. But Lord, I confess this to You today. I realize I have not put You first all these times because You have me covered in Your plans.*

*Holy Spirit, I ask for help to continue to believe in God's plans for my life and future. I pray for the grace to trust and not waver in faith anymore. For even when I walk through the valley of the shadow of death, God will not leave me nor forsake me, in Jesus name.*

## God will heal your heart

**Psalms 9:9** - The LORD also will be a refuge for the oppressed, a refuge in times of trouble.

**Psalms 30:5** - For his anger endures but a moment; in his favor is life: weeping may endure for a night, but joy cometh in the morning.

**Psalm 147:3** - He heals the brokenhearted and binds up their wounds.

### PRAY:

*You, O Lord, are my refuge and fortress in times of trouble. You will protect and keep me safe at all times.*

*Yes, weeping may endure for a night, but joy comes in the morning. I know that my morning of joy is now.*

*O Lord, heal my heart of all forms of brokenness and bind up my wounds. Fill me with joy in place of depression, and confidence in place of anxiety. Make me a pillar of support for those in need, and bring praise to Your name through me, in Jesus name.*

# QUESTIONS

## 1. Are you unhappy about life? What are the things that are making you depressed? List them below

...............................................................

...............................................................

...............................................................

## 2. What will you do today to deal with your unhappiness?

...............................................................

...............................................................

...............................................................

# DECLARATION

*I reject every attack of bitterness on my mind. My joy and happiness is not in the hand of someone else, or in situations, but in my hand; God is with me; He will uphold me with His righteous right hand, and I shall not be moved. I have every reason to be joyful, in the name of Jesus Christ.*

# Chapter 4: A Prayer for Comfort and Emotional Healing

*Heavenly Father, I thank You for Your unending mercies towards me. Thank YOU for caring for me even when I do not know it.*

*Your LOVE towards me is everlasting. I give You praise and honor forever and ever.*

*LORD, even when I'm hurt, YOU care for me. Even when I'm sad and grieved, YOUR love still protects me.*

*You will not allow my soul to perish. Neither will You allow me to be comfortless. For this I say, thank You, LORD.*

*I confess, LORD, that You have not despised nor forgotten me.*

*No matter how grieved and sad I feel, I know that YOU still love me.*

*I know that YOU are working in my life and family to bring to pass, YOUR eternal purpose.*

*I am confident in YOUR work in my life and family.*

*I rest in Your Love and promise, from now, to everlasting.*

---

*LORD Jesus, I call upon you to be my comforter. Let YOUR Spirit comfort and strengthen my inner man.*

*You are my present help in time of need. Heal my broken heart and wounds.*

*Restore unto me the joy of salvation and confidence to proclaim my faith before the world.*

---

*I cast my burden on YOU, O LORD, sustain me and do not allow my faith and spirit to be moved.*

*Lord, You're my refuge in times of trouble and oppression, according to Psalm 9:9. I now ask You, Lord, to deliver me from the pains and problems that oppress me roundabout.*

*Let your plans for peace and hope be made manifest in my heart and mind. Restore my peace, hope, faith, confidence, and purpose, according to Jeremiah 29:11, in Jesus name.*

---

*Jesus, I believe and confess that YOU have delivered me from all my troubles. You have taken away my heaviness of heart and given me joy and confidence.*

*Yes, I have joy; I have faith in the LORD. I have confidence and victory at all times, in Jesus name.*

---

*Holy Spirit, I pray that You guide me through the present situation to respond to people and issues appropriately. Help me to say what I ought to say, how I ought to say it and when I ought to say it. I accept You as my instructor. Please guide and instruct me, in Jesus name*

---

*LORD, lighten my soul for I look unto THEE. Deliver me from misery, hopelessness, and depression. Take away heaviness and shame from me, and deliver me from all my fears, and from all my troubles, for I trust only in YOU.*

*Restore my joy of salvation and cause Your blessings to manifest in my life and household.*

*In Jesus name.*

---

*Even though the young lions do lack, and suffer hunger, because I seek and serve YOU, LORD, cause me not to lack any good thing.*

*My mouth shall be filled with testimony so that I shall declare Your goodness before the brethren.*

*May I bless YOU at all times, and may Your praise continually be in my mouth.*

*Satan, I rebuke you. Whatever seed of depression you have sown in my heart is, at this moment, uprooted in Jesus name.*

*I decree that it is well with my spirit, soul, and body.*

*I decree that my heart is healed and full of praise to the LORD.*

*The joy of the LORD is my strength at all times.*

*I claim my victory over depression, fear, worry, and anxiety.*

*I refuse to be afraid and worry anymore, for the LORD cares for me.*

*He will not let even the very hairs of my head to touch the ground. He will always provide for me.*

*I am forever safe and secure, in Jesus name.*

---

*Thank You, LORD, because Your eyes are upon me and Your ears are open to my prayers.*

*Thank YOU, LORD, for delivering me from all my afflictions.*

*Thank for keeping my bones and soul from being broken.*

*Thank YOU for redeeming my soul from Satan, through the Blood of Jesus Christ.*

*In Jesus Christ name I pray.*

*Amen*

# Declare: "My Help Will Come From Above"

## Psalm 121: 1-8

---

*I will lift up my eyes unto the hills, from whence cometh my help. My help cometh from the Lord, which made heaven and earth.*

*He will not allow my foot to be moved: he that keepeth me will not slumber. Behold, he that keepeth me shall neither slumber nor sleep. The Lord is my keeper: the Lord is my shade upon my right hand.*

*The sun shall not strike me by day, nor the moon by night. The Lord shall preserve me from all evil: he shall protect my soul. The Lord shall protect my going out and my coming in from this time forth, and even for evermore.*

In Jesus name. Amen.

# GOD

# BLESS

# YOU

# Get in Touch

---

We love testimonies.

We love to hear what God is doing around the world as people draw close to Him in prayer.

Please share your story with us.

Also, please consider giving this book a review on Amazon and checking out our other titles at:

amazon.com/author/danielokpara.

Kindly do check out our website at www.BetterLifeWorld.org, and send us your prayer request. As we join faith with you, God's power will be made manifest in your life.

# Other Books by the Same Author

---

1. Prayer Retreat: 21 Days Devotional With Over 500 Prayers & Declarations to Destroy Stubborn Demonic Problems.

2. HEALING PRAYERS & CONFESSIONS

3. 200 Violent Prayers for Deliverance, Healing, and Financial Breakthrough.

4. Hearing God's Voice in Painful Moments

5. Healing Prayers: Prophetic Prayers that Brings Healing

6. Healing WORDS: Daily Confessions & Declarations to Activate Your Healing.

7. Prayers That Break Curses and Spells and Release Favors and Breakthroughs.

8. 120 Powerful Night Prayers That Will Change Your Life Forever.

9. How to Pray for Your Children Everyday

10. How to Pray for Your Family

11. Daily Prayer Guide

12. Make Him Respect You: 31 Very Important Relationship Advice for Women to Make their Men Respect them.

13. How to Cast Out Demons from Your Home, Office & Property

14. Praying Through the Book of Psalms

15. The Students' Prayer Book

16. How to Pray and Receive Financial Miracle

17. Powerful Prayers to Destroy Witchcraft Attacks.

18. Deliverance from Marine Spirits

19. Deliverance From Python Spirit

20. Anger Management God's Way

21. How God Speaks to You

22. Deliverance of the Mind

23. 20 Commonly Asked Questions About Demons

24. Praying the Promises of God

25. <u>When God Is Silent</u>! What to Do When Prayer Seems Unanswered or Delayed

26. <u>I SHALL NOT DIE</u>: Prayers to Overcome the Spirit and Fear of Death.

27. <u>Praise Warfare</u>

28. <u>Prayers to Find a Godly Spouse</u>

29. <u>How to Exercise Authority Over Sickness</u>

30. <u>Under His Shadow:</u> Praying the Promises of God for Protection (Book 2).

# About the Author

Daniel Chika Okpara is an influential voice in contemporary Christian ministry. His vision and mandate are to:

1. Bring others to Christ through the preaching of the Gospel with the demonstration of the power of the Holy Spirit.

2. Establish believers in the Word through real-life teachings, and

3. Empower believers to become Ambassadors of the Kingdom who are bringing others to Christ and Occupying till the Coming of Christ.

He is the founder and CEO of Better Life World Outreach Ministries, a non-denominational ministry committed to global evangelism, and empowering of God's people with insights for victorious living.

He is also the founder of www.BreakthroughPrayers.org , an online portal leading people all over the world to encounter God and change their lives through prayer.

He is the author of over 50 life-transforming books on prayer, faith, entrepreneurship, relationship, and victorious living

WEBSITE: www.betterlifeworld.org

BOOKS:
www.amazon.com/author/danielokpara

# NOTES

•

Printed in Great Britain
by Amazon

38452626R00066